JUSTICE SERIES - VOL 2

STREETS OF JUSTICE

RETURNING TRUTH TO THE PUBLIC SQUARE

STEFFRON T. JAMES

STREETS OF
JUSTICE

ISBN: 978-0-9998144-2-0
ISBN: 978-0-9998144-3-7 (eBook)

Editor: Tosha Jones of JMC Marketing & Communications (tjones@thejmc.com)
Nashville, Tennessee USA

Editor: Helen James
Stone Mountain, Georgia USA

Content Editor: Debra D. Winans of Linking Solutions LLC (linkingdolutions.net)
Atlanta, Georgia USA

Design & Layout: Michael Matulka of Basik Studios (www.gobasik.com)
Omaha, Nebraska USA

Publisher: Kingdom Living Ministries - Publishing (www.thewayofjustice.com)
Murfreesboro, Tennessee USA

Printed in the United States of America

10 9 8 7 6 5 4 3 2 1

"IF WE GET JUSTICE RIGHT, IT WILL RIGHT THE CULTURE"

- Steffron T. James

PREFACE
A FRESH PERSPECTIVE ON JUSTICE

"Of course, I know what justice is!" This is what I would have said a few years ago before I actually delved into the subject. I quickly learned that the concept of justice is vaster than I ever imagined.

In my quest to gain a better understanding of justice, I found two distinct groups of people; justice champions and justice advocates.

In my research, I first discovered justice champions. These tremendous individuals and groups humbled me by their justice acts selflessly delivered to the disenfranchised – the down and out needing a hand up. These justice champions throughout history have sacrificed, given their lives, families, money, time, energy, and passion towards making things better by "putting things right for others." It was easily seen how their efforts put people back in community, helping facilitate their full engagement with the rest of society. They were giving "hands up and not just handouts."

For example, Dr. Martin Luther King Jr, a universal icon of social activism, understood the far-reaching need for justice to be an essential element to life when he said, "Injustice anywhere is a threat to justice everywhere."

The other characteristic that stood out about justice champions is that even though they accomplished extraordinary achievements, they were quite humble and sought no credit or praise for their efforts.

However, just as I was humbled by justice champions, I was bewildered by another group: justice advocates. They talked about justice. They declared themselves just and defenders of justice. However, their efforts yielded very different results. There was usually not a return to the community, and they created more division, more tensions, more animosity, and for sure more blame.

As I studied and observed both groups, I recognized both seemed to have impassioned causes which they called "justice," but the means of going about it were very different. The results of their efforts were even starker.

> *"Men often mistake killing and revenge for justice.*
> *They seldom have the stomach for justice."*
>
> *- Robert Jordan (A Famous American Author)*

When true justice is engaged and adhered to, it is compassionate and redemptive in nature. Jordan realized justice breaks with the norms of natural inclinations. It requires a measured response governed by characteristics not willing to be embraced by many.

> *"Social justice cannot be attained by violence.*
> *Violence kills what it intends to create"*
>
> *- Pope John Paul II*

Illumination began to happen for me, that not all justice is just! Too often some so-called justice endeavors kill what they intend to create. Just naming a thing justice will not bring about justice or ensure we are being just. I also concluded – after some pondering – there had to be criteria applied to our justice acts that would help any effort toward righting wrongs to be done right. Right deserves being done right! Justice should not be used as a simple buzz word. When we conduct any of our affairs on earth towards the rest of humanity, we can't be void of justice criteria.

In this small booklet, hopefully I will provide what I have come to see as necessary justice criteria. My heart's desire is to give a different and alternative perspective, another viewpoint, and additional assistance to help your cause truly help others. *"Evil men do not understand justice, but those who seek the Lord understand it completely"* (Prov 28:5). Do we really understand justice completely? I sure didn't!

So, I humbly request you hang in there and join me on this journey as we unfold justice together!

INTRODUCTION

A desire. A thirst. A longing for significance. These are the catalysts that have compelled me to write a four-part series about the concept of justice.

Over the past four years, I have been taken to school and to task on this subject that I didn't know had relevance to my purpose or destiny in life. I am a believer in God, but this subject is not limited to, nor exclusive to those of like mind. It is a societal issue and need.

I have discovered that justice may be one of the most misunderstood, but beneficial concepts known to man. However, it may possess the opportunity to right many of the ill we face with humanity. Understanding justice and applying its principles can change governments, countries, cities, individuals, and all in between. It is a way to approach life, other people, situations, and circumstances with balance and soundness.

I know what you are thinking; I must be selling some magic pill or potion. I assure you; I was as shocked as any when I began to realize the implications of this subject. I was even more shocked with the overwhelmingly positive responses I got as I began to share it with others. Individuals who I respect and know to be more studious, well-informed, well-read, contemplative, and honestly smarter than me encouraged me to write this four-part series.

My first book, *Champions of Justice*, was very in-depth and technical. The feedback I received was to present the same information in smaller, bite-sized pieces that are easier to digest and embrace. This would allow those who are newly introduced to the concept of justice to truly grasp its implications and understand its impact.

You are about to eat a small meal that will hopefully keep bringing you back to the table. If you want the full-course meal all at once, you can order *Champions of Justice* from our website: *www.thewayofjustice.com.*

I pray the reading of each book (The Cause of Justice, The Streets of Justice, The Path of Justice, and The Way of Justice) will expose you little-by-little to the relevance and necessity of understanding the concept of justice. These books truly give us a culture-changing perspective of justice.

ENJOY THE APPETIZER!

TABLE OF CONTENT

STREETS OF JUSTICE

CHAPTER ONE
BACK TO SCHOOL

"Justice consists not in being neutral between right and wrong, but in finding out the right and upholding it against wrong."

- Theodore Roosevelt

Over the last five years or so, I have been taken to school, I mean; absolutely taken to task personally and by the not so subtle provoking and nudging of the scriptures on the subject of justice. During this time, I have discovered very few individuals, entities, institutions, or establishments truly understand and apply the essence of true justice. But the truth be exposed, neither did I when I started this journey.

From the onset, I truly felt I had a reasonable grasp of justice, only to discover, I had no idea the depth of my ignorance. I made huge assumptions without knowledge, wisdom, insight or understanding. Don't get me wrong, I found many talking about justice and labeling things justice. However, with a little inquiry and investigation, I found the justice that was implied or applied didn't pass the litmus test. I discovered certain criteria had to be in place for true justice to occur.

Most people I found advocating for a cause declared themselves "just," a justice warrior, or a social justice advocate. They were bold, invigorated, and impassioned. Their declarations, however, seemed to resonate a nobility of epic proportions. It was somewhat of a moral trump card giving passage to a type of sainthood. Their cause seemed to be a soapbox insulating them from inquiry, evaluation, scrutiny, and interrogation of their chosen issue to defend, champion, protest, promote, and argue.

Let me make it crystal clear, I have no problem with an impassioned cause. I believe we are all placed on the earth to effect change through a focused, impassioned, purpose in life. But I have become acutely aware, emotionally charged causes are one of the greatest breeding grounds for the miscarriage of justice.

Without a thorough understanding of justice, we may land in what I have come to see as the most dangerous position to be in, The Justice Assumption Zone! The Justice Assumption Zone is when we believe, think, and voice a stand for justice without applying any of the basic characteristics of justice. Let's briefly review a few them.

CHARACTERISTICS OF JUSTICE

Justice is blind, but never deaf. It does not see cause, color, creed, or culture, but it hears restoration to community. Justice asks the question, "how do I get this person back in community or protect the community from oppression in a humble, compassionate and merciful way?" Every man is owed justice; but not every man is just. Though possibly not deserving justice; justice must be applied... regardless! Justice has no partiality.

JUSTICE CRITERIA

In order for transformational justice to occur, a situation must be evaluated using the following three justice criteria.

1. **Equity Position or an Established Equity:** Freedom from bias and favoritism established before an encounter and used during.

2. **Objective Right/Standard/Measure:** No error in intention, talk, or actions; good faith towards the one to whom you stand in judgment; no unjust attempts to be malicious, malign, or mislead.

3. **Deductive Truth:** truth that welcomes interrogation and scrutiny: no pronouns associated with it; not my truth, our truth, their truth...It is *the truth!*

These Justice Characteristics and Criteria are the simple litmus tests that disqualify most causes from legitimately having any mention of "justice" in their title! A cause may be your passion, it may be what drives you, you may have all your energy behind it, but if your justice cause, does not follow these basic guidelines, you may be perverting justice. I am simply asking you to be willing to consider if your justice is producing just results.

One other interesting note here; justice is always about getting individuals back into community. Justice is about creating an environment for those who want to contribute their gifts, talents, and abilities no matter how small and seemingly insignificant. The reality is, not all want to contribute, as sad as that may seem. Justice only ensures just opportunity and exposure for all. Respectfully, justice is a hand up not a handout!

Let me quickly highlight a few things I have discovered about justice in my deep dive to get a fuller grasp of the implications of appropriately applied justice:

- "Justice is the foundation of all that God does in heaven and on earth."

- "Justice is God's radical recalibration strategy for all that is out of order on the earth."

- "Justice is God's standard for man's interactions on the earth."

- "Justice is God's means of *putting things right* on earth."

ARMED WITH THIS INTRODUCTORY GLIMPSE, LET'S KEEP DISCOVERING.

STREETS OF JUSTICE

CHAPTER TWO
THE ELEVATOR ANSWER

Hopefully the introduction and preface have given you a small glimpse into the subject of justice and have whet your appetite to learn more! I will start in this chapter with a definition of justice and why I see it as an essential link to where we are in the 21st century.

I was challenged in Lagos, Nigeria, a couple of years ago by a young man as I was teaching a Bible class on the subject of justice. I was exploring and reviewing scriptures with the group and sharing the importance of justice being included in any serious conversation about needed changes in Africa. The young man raised his hand a little over halfway through the lecture and asked, "how would you define justice?"

I felt I gave a good answer by saying, "it is your opportunity to do just things for others." Then I gave a couple of canned descriptions I had heard in the past about justice.

However, after I left the meeting and thought more about the question, I began to form a much deeper response to the meaning and definition of justice. I began to realize that justice is a key element needed for change, for righting wrongs, for eradicating oppression, and for putting people back in community. I had never fully processed a true definition that captured the fullness of justice. I surmised at that moment that I needed an elevator answer – a quick, 15- second summary – of what would capture the true essence and definition of justice without a full-blown lecture!

"Putting things right!" That was the impetus. It captured the basic concept. But for me, it was necessary to have a far-reaching definition of justice to establish boundaries and to hedge in behaviors, keeping it from being all over the board. Here is where I landed that night after an intense time of pondering:

"JUSTICE IS THE CAPABILITY, MEANS, AND WILLINGNESS TO PUT THINGS RIGHT FOR OTHERS, IN A JUST WAY, FOR THE JUST ONE."

Some of you may become unglued about the last part, "for the just One." I know many people don't believe in God, a higher power, a divine creator, or sovereign entity that initiated all of what we see and don't see. Though one may not believe in any of those things, that doesn't make them any less true and effective. I may not believe in, like or respect the accomplishments of Thomas Edison. However, I still turn on my lights every day.

The truth is, applying the principles of God's word really works! Even if you don't fully appreciate who God is, you can be a beneficiary of His principles. Your feelings and disposition don't stop the principles of justice from working. Justice accomplished using the principles of justice brings about just ends.

Now, let's break down that definition of justice I previously mentioned.

"Justice is the capability, means,
and willingness to put things right for others,
in a just way, for the just One."

Capability: This requires being in a position to effect outcomes. It means having authority. It means having the power to initiate, control, or foster change. By the way, this is often accomplished from the most basic disposition in life.

Means: A president, king, or ruler may have the authority and still lack the means to accomplish the thing needed. Means is not simply being in a power position or having money. It is any position where you can leverage money, people, intellect, skill and heart to accomplish change. Position means little unless we are willing to invest your means to put things right.

You may be a janitor, school teacher, electrician, or secretary and have means. You have gifts and talents. You can be the leader and example to carry everyone to a better place. Means is the capital to perform. Anyone may be the possessor of this capital as mentioned above. For example, Joseph in the Bible did it from the position of slave and prisoner. A slave girl was the deliverer of justice to Naaman. The least likely kid in the class defends a helpless student from being bullied. The kid who was defended, later willingly helps tutor the bully in algebra. Means has purchasing power and value. Means is making available your human capital.

Willingness: This one element is often overlooked. We can want things to be different and want them to change. But will the energy be expended to accomplish a needed endeavor that can put things right? Justice is personal! It requires conviction, courage, involvement, resolve, and often sacrifice to see things get better.

To put things right: Chaos, contention, oppression, injustice, pain, and suffering can be minimized – and in frequent cases eradicated – if true justice is engaged in the situation. Wrongs are present in society. But as the old adage indicates, "two wrongs don't make a right." In order to arrive at "right," there must be a truth, a standard with which to calibrate and measure initiating behaviors and responding behaviors. We put things right when our formula, recipe, and ingredients are right from the onset.

In a just way: This is where the wheels typically come off. "Just way," has been quite subjective. We apply our version of just. We apply our version of pain. We apply our oppression as the identification of what is to be put right. Our truth, our reality, our story becomes the reality from which we launch our impassioned attempts to put things right with others, for others, for the world, for things and circumstances. Shaking our fist often in frustration, we even say, "I will make a difference in spite of God, who doesn't seem to care. How could He care and allow the terrible atrocities of life to occur?"

There is an outcry of desire for equal sharing of wealth, pain, prosperity, opportunity, and suffering. Sadly, we fail to consider the huge varying factors that prevent any hope of true equality in these areas.

LET'S SUMMARIZE

Justice is displayed when an individual – from any position in life – chooses to use his or her means to help put things right for others, put things back in order for others (friend or foe), in a manner that is compassionate, merciful, kind, and makes for peace. And if you believe in God, for the only just One! If you don't believe, it's okay, at least there is a greater opportunity for your justice to be just!

CHAPTER THREE
TRUE JUSTICE EXPOSED

We are all individuals with different personalities, drives, motivations, past experiences, gifts, talents, abilities, and life-shaping events. We are the result of varied external and internal environmental exposures. So, how could we possibly agree to a universal standard of true justice? What is our justice "compass?"

In Chapter 1, we outlined Justice Characteristics and Criteria that must exist for true justice to be possible. Let's explore scriptures that support this idea and delve even deeper.

Take a look with me at the following Scripture:

> [14] *"Justice is turned back, and righteousness stands far away; for truth has stumbled in the public squares, and uprightness cannot enter.* [15] *Truth is lacking, and he who departs from evil makes himself a prey. The LORD saw it, and it displeased him that there was no justice"*
>
> - Isaiah 59:14-15

What an indictment! Justice is turned back. We must grasp this; In our cities, towns, communities, nations, people groups, and tribes, justice is being turned back. Justice is the very thing we are supposed to use as a litmus test for all of our interactions within humanity. Justice is a call to everyone! It is what we are to be doing.

The second element that transpires in this verse is righteousness, the objective measure for our behaviors toward each other. Righteousness is our how. It gives standards for how to do justice. Remember Justice Criteria #2, *objective right/measure/standard* which indicates there is a freedom from malice, maligning, and intent to mislead. There is no ill will, there is good faith toward all, no deceit, no corruption, no bribes, and no compromise of *right*.

Look at the next statement in Isaiah 59:14. "Truth has stumbled..."!
Truth has tripped in the public square. Actually, it has face planted.
Without the truth, we are void of necessary information to make
proper evaluation. Your truth seeking has to be deductive (Justice
Criteria #3), not inductive. Truth charges us to not dictate what it
reveals. Truth is discovering not what we want, but what is. We
can't form our own conclusion and look for verification.

Unfortunately, "truth" in many cases has become what we want and
believe to be true based on our experience. That is totally subjective.
Though I am quoting and using scriptures, these elements are not
just about the church, but the effects of God's kingdom on the world.
(Let me not get ahead of myself, that's another book!) Judgment
starts at the church (God's people), then spills into the streets with
all people. I will show you that truth in a moment.

Zion, the church, as God's people are culpable, but so are those in
the streets (the public square). We are told in Zechariah 7:9 (NKJV)
"...*Execute true justice...*"! So, there is a justice that can appear true,
but lacks the needed characteristics or criteria to cut the mustard.
Justice invites truth that might not yet be known or is yet to be
experienced by you individually. In other words, you seek for truth;
you don't make snap judgments without all the information and facts.
Justice demands the truth. We must welcome interrogation and
scrutiny of our truth for justice to prevail.

The "public square" is all encompassing, but each area of it is
desperate for justice to be embraced by a few courageous souls.
It refers to business, government, education, military, media,
entertainment, sports, etc.

"Uprightness" is mentioned next in Isaiah 59:14. This is our equity
portion, also defined in Justice Criteria #1. Freedom from bias
and favoritism. Equity cannot get on the street where you live. We
all have people who dislike us. They may even disagree with us
politically, religiously and philosophically. There can easily be other
issues causing an absence of our mutual fond feelings such as:
color, cause, culture or creed. But the question is, "does that person
have any chance of you being objective in your justice approach
to them?" If not, then uprightness has no chance on your street!

Many times, we show justice to family, friends, favorites, and those we fancy, even when they are not just. Uprightness requires just treatment of the not so fond of. Remember, the feelings might be mutual. Both deserve your just uprightness.

STREETS OF JUSTICE

CHAPTER FOUR
STREET JUSTICE

Poor race relations in America seem to be at an all-time high considering more strides have been made to make them better than any time in history (evidenced by America recently electing its first black president for two terms). This in no way means there are no racial injustices. Yet, Dr. Martin Luther King Jr., and others who fought for the justice of black people, would have rejoiced to see this day and celebrated the progress made.

But what happens when a member of the black community expresses a different perspective from what are generally accepted or "approved" ideas? For example, what if an African American voted for Barack Obama's political opponent? Would those who previously sought justice become the unjust?

The attacks I have heard and seen against any dissenter from certain black narratives or even any black person who would dare question the absolute sainthood of former president Barrack Obama or articulate the progress made, have often been viciously accused of being "uncle Tom, coon, sellout, plantation n****), just to give a few.

These attacked individuals subscribe to a different narrative. Not ignoring the potential for racism, not ignoring a dark past of intense racial disparity, but now these "sell outs" are taking personal responsibility for their own choices and outcomes without blaming others for their dispositions in life. They have been given opportunity. They don't need a handout, just a hand up and now that they can walk for themselves; they want to learn to run, but they don't need anyone to run for them. They recognize evil is in the world in all forms, with racism as one of them. However, the more profound effect on their individual success is contingent upon their own choices, responses, and efforts in life; they take control of their own destiny!

Making these types of declarations quite often invite a lashing; you become "a prey." The same occurs when it comes to a cause someone happens to feel very strongly about. It is as if, when you are not in agreement with the same level of emotion, viewpoint, and critical nature of the "group's, crew's, creed's, culture's, and tribe's" assertion then you have lost your right to be human. Or at least you are to be dismissed as in-humane and therefore, irrelevant as a person or individual that deserves the least consideration for any just treatment. There is a term for that behavior; it's called self-righteous or moral superiority.

In Chapter 3, we read Isaiah 59:14. The next verse begins by saying, *"Truth is lacking, and he who departs from evil makes himself a prey."* First let me highlight this behavior is called "evil." Someone finally sees the error of his ways; he has been mocking, perverting, or doing injustice to a certain group. He has been biased, non-objective, and living a lie toward humanity. He has been more concerned about self-preservation, self-promotion of his cause and group, or self-indulgent than seeing his role in the human condition. Then finally, he decides to make a change.

On cue, obliteration comes for breaking rank with the herd, with the crowd, with the "crew," and with his fellow cause advocates. Matthew 12:18 says, *"Woe unto you scribes, Pharisees, hypocrites; you tithed mint, and cumin, and dill and neglect the weightier matters of justice, mercy, and faithfulness."*

Leave your complacency. Leave the masses with a newfound level of virtue. Leave your tribe and creed and see how they treat you. You often are labeled a sellout. I am just bringing awareness, so when you are attacked for it, know that it is not unusual!

The second part of Isaiah 59:15 says, *"The LORD saw it, and it displeased him that there was no justice."* It should displease us as a people also. We all have a responsibility when it comes to justice. We are to do it, give it, establish it, execute it, observe it, promote it, uphold it, grant it, and even sing about it…and we will! Check out these two scriptures.

*¹ "Run to and fro through the streets of
Jerusalem, look and take note! Search her squares
to see if you can find a man, one who does justice
and seeks truth, that I may pardon her."*

- Jeremiah 5:1

The second is an acceptance of the call to all humanity, the assignment to all humanity, to return to justice.

*⁶ "So you, by the help of your God,
return, hold fast to love and justice,
and wait continually for your God"*

- Hosea 12:6

This is where the title of this booklet originated. If you combine the Isaiah 59:14-15 and the Jeremiah 5:1 scriptures, our streets are to be "Streets of Justice," truth is to return to the public square, which is every area of interaction with another person. The public square can be your neighborhood, your business, your school, your church, your anything. We need a fresh perspective on justice.

A study of biblical history reveals, Jerusalem stands out as a type and shadow for any city, any place in the world. As is spoken concerning Jerusalem - for the most part - the same can be ascribed to all cities, with the exception of historical precedence and actual events. Jerusalem can be an example of any city in the world, especially the church world.

A couple of other names for the city of Jerusalem are Zion, the City of David, Jebus, Salem, and the city of heaven. There are others, but you get the point. Whenever God is speaking of redemption, restoration, and recovering His people from error or apostasy, He gives instructions and principles that can be considered universally applicable for any people wanting radical reformation in their lives or cities. *"If my people which are called by my name would humble themselves and pray..."* (2 Chronicles 7:14). This is universal!

> [18] *"You shall appoint judges and officers in all your towns that the LORD your God is giving you, according to your tribes, and they shall judge the people with righteous judgment.* [19] *You shall not pervert justice. You shall not show partiality, and you shall not accept a bribe, for a bribe blinds the eyes of the wise and subverts the cause of the righteous.* [20] *Justice, and only justice, you shall follow, that you may live and inherit the land that the LORD your God is giving you"*
>
> *- Deuteronomy 16:18–20*

> [27] *"Zion shall be redeemed by justice, and those in her who repent, by righteousness"*
>
> *- Isaiah 1:27*

> [5] *"He appointed judges in the land in all the fortified cities of Judah, city by city,* [6] *and said to the judges, "Consider what you do, for you judge not for man but for the LORD. He is with you in giving judgment.* [7] *Now then, let the fear of the LORD be upon you. Be careful what you do, for there is no injustice with the LORD our God, or partiality or taking bribes*
>
> *- 2 Chronicles 19:5-7*

This is just a brief sample of scriptures that can be applied universally, and the same principles – if engaged at any time in history – yield the same results.

For example, let's try a quick exercise where you insert words into Jeremiah 5:1 below that best apply to you personally.

"Run to and fro throughout the streets of (**your city**). Look and take note (**recognize something that is noteworthy**)! Search her squares (**look not just in the church, but in the streets and places of everyday people of the city, in business, government, schools, entertainment, military, etc.**) to see if you can find one who does justice and seeks truth. (**Why? This type of person will cause the entire city to be pardoned.**)"

Remember our scripture from Isaiah 59:14 *"Justice has been turned back."* If a just and truth-seeking person(s) can be located, the city has hope. The city where you live may be dark, it may have all types of issues, but I want to let you know justice can turn it around. Love is needed, but justice operating with the right criteria opens the door for love to be experienced.

> [3] *"Blessed are those who observe justice and do righteousness at all times"*
>
> *- Psalm 106:3*

Notice the verse says, "observe justice" and continues with "do righteousness at all times." These two actions are always partnered though having different aspects. Justice is *what* we do; righteousness is *how* we do it. Justice is the standard; righteousness is the calibration of the standard.

I have discovered that justice is rarely on the radar of the best of us. As I said earlier, we speak about various forms of social and criminal justice. However, as a part of the fabric of society and our daily interaction, I am sad to say we are sorely missing the mark. We leave justice to others.

In verse three of Psalm 106, the word "blessed" means having all that is needed, having full supply, happiness of circumstance, and joyful peace of mind. *Blessed means having all needed for full and abundant supply.* Is it possible we miss being blessed because we are missing justice?

STREETS OF JUSTICE

CHAPTER FIVE
YOUR JUSTICE
MUST BE JUST

God said, *"I will make justice the line and righteousness the plum line, hail will sweep away the refuge of lies, and water will overwhelm the shelters"* (Isaiah 28:17).

When justice is the line, the definitive, the absolute, the core guide, the operating mode, then lies have no place, bribes have no place, partiality has no place, and corruption has no place. When righteousness is your plum line standard, there is no ill intent, no maliciousness or malice, only good faith toward the person you are engaging in life. You have clean hands (how you deal with and handle others) and a clean heart (your intent behind your dealings).

When righteousness is your plum line, the water mentioned in Isaiah 28:17 refers to the refreshing and cleansing that will come to areas where injustice, oppression, and wrong have made their dwelling. Justice and righteousness are equal partners though different in function and application.

I want to reintroduce one other concept at this juncture that can't be ignored when discussing true justice: Equity; not equality, but equity.

Equity is the justice and righteousness standard. Equity is the umbrella and common denominator for a justice and righteousness partnership. *Equity: freedom from bias and favoritism.* Equity ensures your foes, those you are fighting, those you want to forget, even those you might consider fools get justice. Equity commands an established standard where you don't pervert justice for your family, friends, nor favorites. Equity is pre-situational. It is a predetermined behavior adhered to before a situation arises.

Oftentimes, we have no inkling what we might face. Equity gives us a right outlook to have, so the perplexing situation doesn't lead to unjust actions. Justice and righteousness require equity regardless of circumstances!

Justice must be blind. Therefore, it can't look at creed, color, culture, or cause in its application. Justice has to be applied with equity in spite of emotion, if not, foundations are broken down and nothing can be trusted. Justice has to become your vindicating light!

None of us have the luxury of waiting on others to do justice. We have to be like the "Good Samaritan" in Luke chapter 10 who acted immediately to help a stranger even when others had chosen not to. In Luke 10:25, a lawyer asks Jesus, *"what must I do to gain eternal life?"* At the end of a lengthy discourse, Jesus told the lawyer, *"you go do likewise."*

Like many of us, this guy wanted to know what he must do to get to heaven, to see the next life, to gain passage to what he felt would be next.

Keeping the commandments was the first thing, which the lawyer assured Jesus he was doing. Next, the lawyer said it was required to love God with all your heart, soul, mind and strength, which he was also doing. But then came this little statement, "love your neighbor as yourself." The lawyer then asked Jesus, "who is my neighbor?"

The rest of the story was a parable with four characters. All of the individuals were on a road between the city of Jerusalem and a town called Jericho. The first man on the road fell prey to thieves who robbed, beat, and left him for dead.

Next is a priest who comes down the road and sees the helpless injured man and moves quickly past on the other side of the road. Priests are considered those who represent God on earth.

Then a Levite comes by and he also passes by and continues without offering any assistance to the man who was robbed. Levites are those who are servants of God known for their sacrifice as helpers.

Last, a Samaritan on a journey sees the injured man and comes to his aide. He bandages his wounds, puts him on his donkey and takes him to an inn. He cares for him until he has to leave. He then leaves funds with the inn keeper to continue the man's care until he's well, conveying if any additional cost is incurred, he, the Samaritan, would pay the bill on his next journey.

Jesus asks the lawyer, "who do you think was the neighbor?"

"The Samaritan," the lawyer says. Jesus having depicted an undeniable conclusion said, "you go do likewise." Though the care shown by the Samaritan is a tremendous example of being a neighbor. It has a more profound implication. You see, the Samaritan and the injured man (a Jew) are not neighbors; they are enemies. The Jews call the Samaritans dogs. Jesus is saying you go be that kind of "dog" to someone else!

DOING JUSTICE DOES NOT DISTINGUISH CULTURE, COLOR, CREED, OR CAUSE; IT CAN'T AFFORD TO.

Four people were going down the road, either could have been five minutes earlier and ended up being the injured man. As long as we all "do likewise," it shouldn't matter. But if we aren't doing likewise, how can you safely walk down any road?

"Love your neighbor as yourself." The conversation between Jesus and the lawyer concluded with the thought that to have eternal life, an individual has to resemble, model, and exemplify the term neighbor.

"Neighbor" launched a clarification parable with staggering implications. The conclusion? If you want eternal life, then, "go do likewise!"

Being the "Samaritan type of neighbor" demonstrated the essence of both eternal life and true love. The Samaritan willingly used his *capability and means to put things right for another;* he was just!

Hosea says, "return." Return from what? Your lack of justice and love shown to others! Take a look at the verse.

> [6] *"So you, by the help of your God,*
> *return, hold fast to love and justice,*
> *and wait continually for your God."*
>
> *- Hosea 12:6*

It says you will need the help of God for this return. From the earlier verse Isaiah 59:14, justice has been turned back, justice has been squashed in the public square.

> [7] *"For the vineyard of the LORD of hosts*
> *is the house of Israel, and the men of Judah are*
> *his pleasant planting; and he looked for justice,*
> *but behold bloodshed; for righteousness,*
> *but behold an outcry!"*
>
> *- Isaiah 5:7*

Justice and righteousness have been replaced, truth has stumbled in the public square, in our streets. But there is hope! We can return and with the help of our God, holdfast to justice and love and wait continually upon our God! *"...for the Lord is a God of Justice and blessed are all those who wait for Him."* (Isaiah 30:18b)

I almost titled this booklet *Sons and Daughters of Justice* because of what was revealed by this next scripture. The Patriarch Abraham was called to be a blessing to the nations. His call was not just to his immediate natural descendents. The scripture concludes any who are of faith are blessed with the same promises of Abraham. Therefore, any who are of faith are Abraham's seed and seeds of the same promises. But what was the promise of Abraham based upon? Was it just faith? Faithfulness? Some act of faith alone? Or, was it faith in a specific foundational principle?

> [19] *"For I have chosen him, that he may*
> *command his children and his household after him*
> *to keep the way of the LORD by doing righteousness*
> *and justice, so that the LORD may bring to Abraham*
> *what he has promised him."*
>
> *- Genesis 18:19*

Did you get that? God chose Abraham under a condition. What was the condition? That he commanded/taught his children sons and daughters and his household coming after him to keep the "way of the Lord," by doing righteousness and justice. The way of the Lord according to this verse is "righteousness and justice."

Look at the last line of the scripture; "…So that the Lord may bring to Abraham what He (The Lord) has promised him (Abraham). All the promises of Abraham: to be a father of many nations, that every piece of land his feet step on was his, that his seed would be as numerous as the stars of heaven and the sand of the sea shore, that riches and honor would be his inheritance are all contingent upon teaching his sons and daughters (household) following him "righteousness and justice."

As a confirmation to what was said about justice in the previous verse about Abraham, take a look at this verse…

> *⁴ "The Rock, his work is perfect, for all his ways are justice. A God of faithfulness and without iniquity, just and upright is he."*
>
> *- Deuteronomy 32:4*

> *⁷ "But the Lord sits enthroned forever, He has established His throne for justice."*
>
> *- Psalm 9:7*

All of God's ways are just. His throne, which is forever, is established for justice. Just and upright (righteous) is He! We are to be no less just to see things turn in society. In Genesis 1:26, God created us in His image and likeness. Our image is to be one of justice! We need a paradigm shift. We must amend our ways if we are to be sons and daughters of justice!

Listen, we will never eradicate the ills and injustices of the world by focusing on the evils of others or the ills themselves. The only hope we have is *being* and *doing* good ourselves.

[10] "For we are His workmanship created in Christ Jesus for good works, which God prepared beforehand, that we should walk in them."

- Ephesians 2:10 (Emphasis mine)

[17] "learn to do good; seek justice, correct oppression; bring justice to the fatherless, plead the widow's cause."

- Isaiah 1:17

[15] "Hate evil, and love good, and establish justice in the gate..."

- Amos 5:15a

Everyone has a choice in situations daily, like the Samaritan, to execute or administer justice to some we like and to some who traditionally we may have hated and they perhaps despised us. If we are going to be a light to nations, we must shine in the face of darkness, in spite of darkness. It is not enough to declare yourself a justice advocate or social justice warrior. Good has to began to look good on you!

[5] "The Lord within her (each oppressing city or person) is righteous, He does no injustice, every morning He shows forth His justice, each dawn He does not fail, but the unjust know no shame."

- Zephaniah 3:5

I must say this again, your justice must be just! God is showing up looking for someone who will execute justice on His behalf. If we'd be truly honest with ourselves, it is the departure from acts of justice in just ways that has led to the deterioration of our homes, neighborhoods, streets, and cities. There is no shortage of causes, that's for sure. However, no one wants to get involved or expend the necessary energy to help. And when help is rendered occasionally, it comes with agendas and strings attached that sabotage the effort.

It is easy to recognize how much danger there is in the streets of many of our cities. All recognize that corruption runs rampant in countless circles. We see the blatant disregard for human decency and genuine care. But do we give up on our obligation to put things right in our cities? I assure you, if good people do nothing, evil will prevail and eventually show up at our doorsteps.

STREETS OF JUSTICE

CHAPTER SIX
GIVE ME A HEART
TO DISCERN JUSTICE

"Learn to do good; seek justice…" is written in Isaiah 1:17. It seems strange the writer has to give such a simple instruction to an entire nation of people. It is as if they had lost this basic human trait. It was no longer second nature. I would submit, based on historical data, basic goodness had ceased to be in large part present in their societal make up. Sounds familiar doesn't it?

The hearts of many have grown cold and callused to others. And beyond that, there are vicious attacks hurled at others for the simplest offense, disagreement, driving infraction, cause dissention, or varying view. There is no tenderness, mercy, compassion or care for the plight of others.

Isaiah 1:19 says; *"if you are willing and obedient (**to verse seventeen, the result is…**) you will eat/have the good of the land."* The writer of this passage understood something so basic, something we must grasp. Without justice our lands can't produce or at least not produce as good or its best.

> [23] *"The uncultivated field of the poor would yield much food, but it is swept away through injustice."*
>
> *- Proverbs 13:23*

Proverbs 22:2 adds this little nugget: *"The poor and the rich meet together, God made them both."*

All people have something to offer to our communities. None of us should treat the rich in an unjust manner, not even to assist the poor. None of us should cater to the rich and despise the poor. Both have value and deserve justice from God's viewpoint. If you rob from the rich to give to the poor, you are a thief. If you only show consideration to the rich because of what you might receive, you have become a respecter of persons, judgmental, and poverty awaits you. There has to be a standard operating procedure for all.

I hear you questioning, "what about love?" Love is necessary, but how many of you would agree that "love" can be faked, perverted, misinterpreted, emotional, and it is a heart issue that is hard to quantify. We need love. When all else fails, love will still stand strong. But even love must be genuine, having appropriate behaviors and characteristics. Love has facets such as discipline, correction, and punishment that often can be mischaracterized by the receiver. Justice has criteria which can be objectively assessed regardless. As I said earlier, the world needs love, but justice is what is required for love to be experience.

Please indulge me as I share five scriptures and bring this to a close. Hopefully it has stirred your hunger for more. I sure pray it has!

> [7] *"The path of life is level for those who are right with God; LORD, you make the way of life smooth for those people.* [8] *But, LORD, we are waiting for your way of justice. Our souls want to remember you and your name.* [9] *My soul wants to be with you at night, and my spirit wants to be with you at the dawn of every day. When your way of justice comes to the land, people of the world will learn the right way of living."*
>
> - Isaiah 26:7-9 (NCV)

> [4] *"Give attention to me, my people, and give ear to me my nation; for a law will go out from me, and I will set my justice for a light to the people."*
> (nations-every people group)
>
> - Isaiah 51:4

*1 "If you return, O Israel, declares the LORD,
to me you should return. If you remove your
detestable things from my presence, and do not
waver, 2 and if you swear, 'As the LORD lives,
'in truth, in justice, and in righteousness, then
nations shall bless themselves in him,
and in him shall they glory."*

- Jeremiah 4:1-2

*8 "He has told you, O man, what is good;
and what does the LORD require of you but
to do justice, and to love kindness, and
to walk humbly with your God?"*

- Micah 6:8

*16 "These are the things you shall do:
Speak each man the truth to his neighbor; render
justice in your gates that makes for peace."*

- Zechariah 8:16 (NKJV)

When you read these accounts of justice described and encouraged by different writers at various times, seasons, and circumstances in the Bible, what conclusion do you draw? Has justice been overlooked? Has justice been neglected as Matthew 23:23 says? Is there an understanding and education on justice needed in the body of Christ and in the world at large? How can you read these verses and not conclude at least a curious inquiry into the subject is needed?

Often, I hear people talking of empowering others through some type of presentation or message. This is never my intent. I don't feel I have that ability. I feel the ability to empower is a God-sized feat reserved for God alone. Hopefully, you are still tracking with me. I have asked God to help me clearly share what He reveals to me about justice. I have also asked for opportunities to expose others to the characteristics of true justice. For me, it has been a tremendous opportunity to learn, be educated, and be provoked to explore at a deeper level based on my hunger and thirst. I invite the same for anyone who has graced me by reading these pages.

I see the subject of justice to be like gold hidden by God for our time. For any who will mine the depths of God for a true understanding of justice, God will release His gold! Check out this powerful word to Solomon, thought to be one of the richest men to ever live, if not *the* richest.

> [11] *"Then God said to him, Because you have asked this thing, and have not asked long life for yourself, nor have asked riches for yourself, nor have asked the life of your enemies, but have asked for yourself understanding to discern justice,* [12] *behold, I have done according to your words; see, I have given you a wise and understanding heart, so that there has not been anyone like you before you, nor shall any like you arise after you.* [13] *And I have also given you what you have not asked: both riches and honor, so that there shall not be anyone like you among the kings all your days."*
>
> *- 1 Kings 3:11-13 (NJKV)*

God told Solomon, "Because you have asked this thing, a heart to discern justice, I have also given you what you have not asked: both riches and honor." I truly believe if anyone takes God at His word and incorporates his/her faith with it, then anyone can be empowered with all that's necessary for justice in the earth! That is what I find in scripture and what I hope happens from your exposure to these powerful dynamics of justice.

Justice is on the heart of God. Justice is the foundation of all God does. Justice is the way of God. Justice is the path of God. Justice is what God is after from us. Justice is a God-sized strategy to put things right on the earth before Jesus' return! If you draw a different conclusion, then I am open to listen and dialogue together.

Look back at what Isaiah 26:9 says out of the New Century Version of the Bible.

> [9] *"My soul wants to be with you at night, and my spirit wants to be with you at the dawn of every day.*

*When your way of justice comes to the land, people
of the world will learn the right way of living."*

- Isaiah 26:9 (NCV)

"People of the world will learn the right way of living." Remember from chapter 1, "Justice is God's radical recalibration of all that is out of order in the earth." I've often heard people say, "the world is a mess," "the world is going to hell in a hand basket," "people are turning more and more toward evil," and one of the most damning, "there is no real hope." I disagree wholeheartedly! There is a plan of redemption, there has always been a plan of redemption! If Jerusalem, after all the destruction and hopeless plights it experienced could again be a shining beacon, then so can the rest of the cities and ultimately the world. As goes Jerusalem, so goes the rest.

*²⁷ "Zion shall be redeemed (rescued, brought back
to life, again be full of all that is good) by justice."*

- Isaiah 1:27

A couple of scriptures out of the list of five I mentioned contained some words I want to bring to your attention. Words like kindness, humility, peace, truth, and righteousness. There are also two other words that often show up as companions of justice; mercy and compassion. Justice has a standard! Learning that standard ensures your justice is just! Your justice being just brings about the promises associated with justice.

This intense booklet has been published to be salt if allowed. It is designed to hopefully get you a little thirsty. My intention was your exposure, expectantly hopeful to have you decide to explore justice at a deeper level, so your mind can be blown like mine was!

You will determine if my effort was successful. How will I know? Acts of justice will begin exploding in the land, in cities, in neighborhoods as normal everyday individuals become "justice champions!" Those who get it will become community lights who establish, enforce, render, and execute justice in their environments.

JUSTICE, GOD'S RADICAL RECALIBRATION STRATEGY FOR ALL THAT IS OUT OF ORDER IN THE EARTH!"

How will we know the message is out? Our speech will betray us, wisdom and justice will govern our tongues. Our steps will be sure and not slip, because the law of God will rule our hearts. That law of God is "justice and love." (Matt 23:23 & Luke 11:42) The world is waiting for us to be a light! Keep this in mind as you go forward, *Justice is always others focused*, so stay focused!

God's not done with the earth nor us. Justice accomplished by these community lights will not be perverted nor a vague form of unidentifiable justice, meeting none of its distinguishing criteria. There will be a wave of *true justice acts* that are redeeming and put individuals back in community as contributors and suppliers to the good of humanity. Decide to be an upholder of justice and it will uphold you! Learn and use the justice criteria:

1. Equity Position

2. Objective Measure

3. Deductive Truth

TRUE JUSTICE IS A MUST FOR US!

Thank you for taking this journey with me;
for together, we are indeed

CHAMPIONS OF JUSTICE!

STREETS OF JUSTICE

ABOUT THE AUTHOR
STEFFRON T. JAMES

Steffron T. James is a South Carolina native. He has made Tennessee his home for the past 17 years. He fondly refers to Tennessee as "the place where God lives." He served our country 22 1/2 years in the US Air Force. He enjoys real estate as his fun day job. Business development and entrepreneurship intrigue him, and he loves teaching and applying sound business practices in various aspects of life. Steffron's greatest passion is teaching the Word of God while challenging individuals to personal development and aspiring to their fullest potential. He is the author of Champions of Justice, the companion book to this one. His five children, three grandchildren, and a multitude of spiritual sons and daughters keep him young and enjoying life.

For more information visit: *www.thewayofjustice.com*

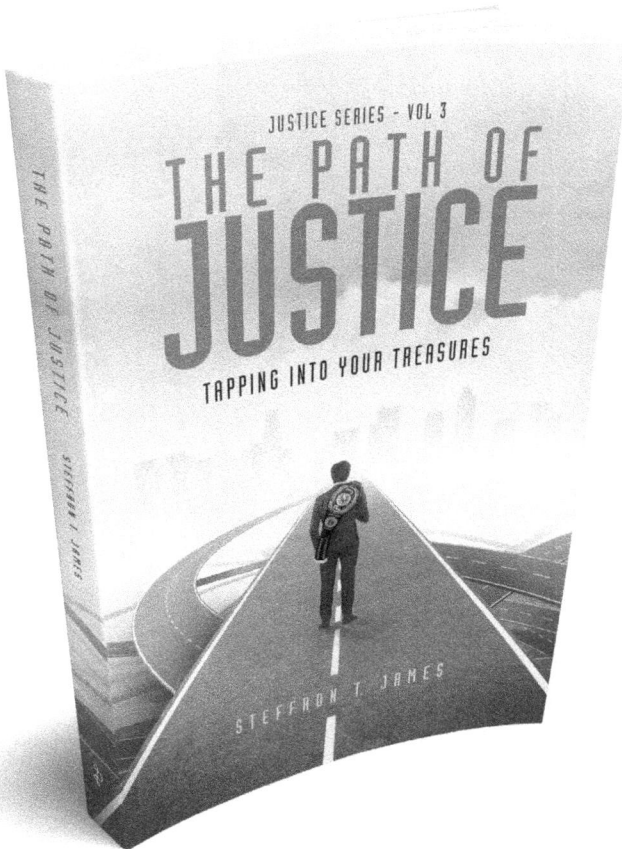

JUSTICE SERIES - VOL 4

THE WAY OF
JUSTICE

THE GAME CHANGER

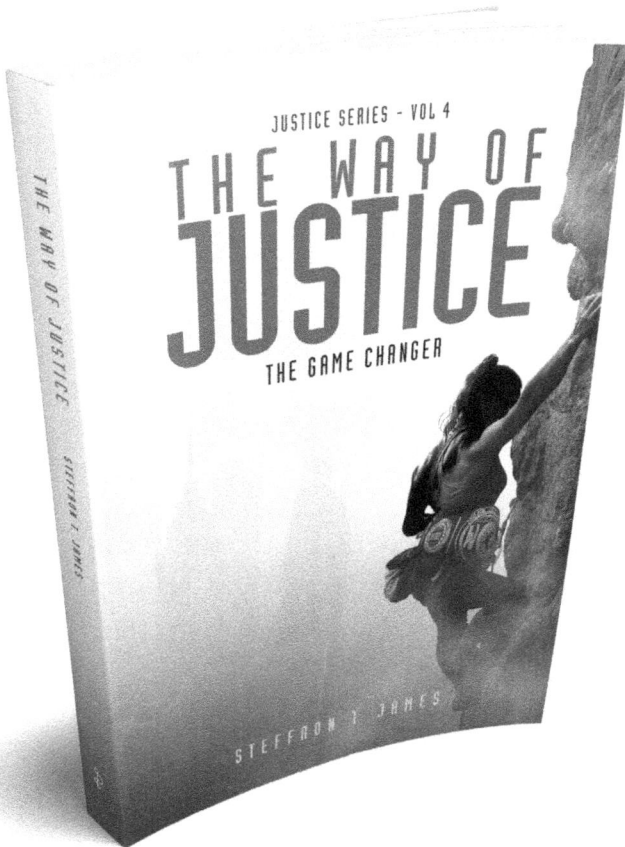

JUSTICE SERIES - VOL 4

THE WAY OF
JUSTICE
THE GAME CHANGER

STEFFRON T JAMES

Available at *www.thewayofjustice.com*

CHAMPIONS OF JUSTICE

DIVINE EMPOWERMENT
FOR WEALTH

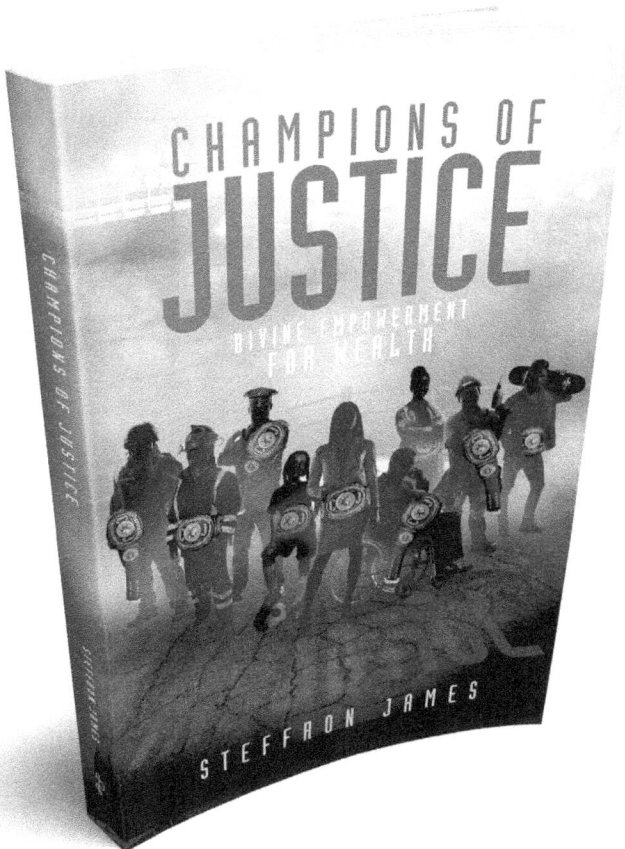

Available at *www.thewayofjustice.com*

JUSTICE SERIES - VOL 2

STREETS OF JUSTICE

RETURNING TRUTH TO THE PUBLIC SQUARE

STEFFRON T. JAMES